To my dearest Joshua, lets see what yo

Love, Auntie

Caroline. xoxoxo.

W9-ATT-658

# Gymnastics

## Monica Phelps

## Contents

2 Introducing Gymnastics
4 Rhythmic Sportive Gymnastics
5 Sports Acrobatics
6 Artistic Gymnastics
9 First Things First
12 Gymnastics Exercises
17 Shaping Up

21 Basic Skills
25 Progressions
26 Jumping and Landing
28 Swinging and Climbing
29 Gym Safety
30 Going Further
32 Index

## Photography by Eileen Langsley

The publishers would like to thank all those who gave their assistance in making
this book, especially Vicky Gofton, Cheryl Hawker, Ashley Howell, Sophie Johnston, Catherine Penny, Geoffrey Penny,
Teresa Penny, Andrew Rattly, Julie Roger, Stewart Struthers and Paul Walsh.

Gym clothes by Carite.

# INTRODUCING GYMNASTICS

To most people, the word gymnastics means exercise and fast, clever movements. In fact, it is an activity you started practising a long time ago. Then it was called play. But every time you run, jump, climb or stretch you are using your physical skills and making gymnastic movements. Of course, to be a gymnast, like those shown on television, means years of hard training. But many people enjoy gymnastics for fun and it helps them to be fit, strong and supple.

## About this book

This book will tell you a little about how gymnastics started and how it has changed over the years. It will show you some gymnastics exercises that you can try at home. Then, if you decide you would like to be a gymnast, there are lots of tips about how to choose a club, what to wear, what to expect, training and gym safety.

## The history of gymnastics

The first gymnasts came from Greece, about three thousand years ago. Games were an important part of everyday life and the boys and young men took part in the sports of the time, such as running, jumping, throwing and wrestling.

It was uncomfortable to play energetic games in normal clothes, so they used to undress themselves. The Greek word for naked is *gymnos* and so the unclothed athletes became known as *gymnasts* and their activities *gymnastics*. As the Greek and then Roman empires declined in importance so did the physical games.

## Pioneers of gymnastics

For many centuries, there was little interest in gymnastics. Then in 1812 a German, Friedrich Ludwig Jahn, started a gymnastics school and invented some apparatus for the gymnasts to use. From this, some of the skills that we now call Artistic Gymnastics developed.

At about the same time in Sweden, Pierre Ling founded a style of gymnastics which became known as Swedish drill. Groups of people did exercises, a bit like people do aerobics today.

A German gymnastic display in Paris in the nineteenth century.

# RHYTHMIC SPORTIVE GYMNASTICS

This is one of the three types of gymnastics seen in competition today. It is a sport for girls in which the gymnast performs an athletic dance sequence, with leaps, jumps and turns set to suitable music. At the same time she has to throw and catch a piece of hand apparatus with the skill of a juggler.

Rhythmic gymnasts can compete on their own or as a group of six. Usually the gymnasts have to perform four exercises using four of the five different pieces of apparatus. Until 1956, the group exercise was included in the Olympic Games in the same programme as artistic gymnastics (see page 6). Since then, it has been recognized as a sport in its own right.

There are five different pieces of hand apparatus that can be used: a rope, ball, hoop, club or ribbon.

# SPORTS ACROBATICS

For many centuries gymnastic skills like acrobatics, or tumbling, were only kept alive by small groups of travelling entertainers and then, later, by circus performers. Now, sports acrobatics is recognized as a branch of gymnastics for both boys and girls, with its own World Championships. In competition it is divided into two main areas.

## Pair and group work

The first area is for pairs or groups, with sections for women's pairs, women's trio (a group of three), men's pairs, men's group of four and mixed pairs.

The gymnasts perform an action-packed sequence, in which they throw and catch each other, balance on each other and perform tumbling tricks. The exercise is carefully worked out so that each movement flows into the next. It is performed to music on a floor measuring 12 metres by 12 metres.

## Tumbling for individuals

The second area is for individuals. The gymnast displays acrobatic skills, with twists and somersaults, one after another, travelling in a straight line, on a tumble run. In competition the person who demonstrates the most difficult tricks will win, as long as they are performed tidily.

For the spectator, this is a thrilling sport to watch and the variety of acrobatic skills creates a 'circus' atmosphere.

# ARTISTIC GYMNASTICS

This is the sort of gymnastics that most people have seen on television.   The gymnast performs routines made from gymnastic skills linked together.  The aim is to perform the most difficult moves perfectly on the different pieces of apparatus.  Women have to compete on four pieces of apparatus and men on six.

Artistic gymnastics is really an event for the individual gymnast.  To succeed  you have to master skills on every piece of apparatus to a  very high standard.  In competition the marks from each exercise are added together to give a total score.

There are, however, team competitions. A team of six gymnasts perform, one at a time, on each of the pieces of  apparatus. Only the best five scores for each exercise count and they are added together to give the team score.  In the Olympic Games and World Champion-ships, the team members also compete in the individual events.

Before the competition the gymnasts have a chance to practise in the arena, so both the men's and women's apparatus are out ready for use.

# The women's apparatus

**Broad horse:** Women vault across the horse.

**Uneven bars:** The gymnasts perform around and over both bars.

**Floor:** Women work to music in an area 12m by 12m.

**Beam:** It is only 10cm wide and almost 5m in length.

# The men's apparatus

**Parallel bars:** The men swing on their hands between them.

**High bar:** The gymnasts swing round a single bar.

**Rings:** An apparatus for strength. The rings must not swing.

**Long Horse:** Men vault along the horse.

**Pommel Horse:** Men swing on the handles on the top of the horse.

**Floor:** The men do not perform to music.

# FIRST THINGS FIRST

## Choosing a club

The first thing to do is to find out what clubs there are in your area. Ask your P.E. teacher at school, look in the local newspaper or on the notice boards at the public library and the sports centre. Then go and see as many different classes as you can so that you can choose one that suits you.

## What to look for

It is wise to find out if the person who is teaching you is properly qualified and if the club is registered with the British Amateur Gymnastics Association (B.A.G.A.). Ask if the club takes part in competitions or if there is an award scheme so that you can take tests to gain your badges if this interests you.

## What to wear

You can wear any clothes as long as they are comfortable and you can move easily in them. Remember, your teacher will need to see the line of your body to check that you are standing properly.

A tracksuit is useful to put on over your gym clothes, to keep you warm.

Stretchy clothes like leotards for girls, and shorts and a vest for boys are suitable.

## Footwear

It is best to start gymnastics barefoot. When you need gymnastics slippers, your coach will advise you on the type to buy and where to get them.

## Hair and jewellery

Your hair should be tied back from your face so that you can see properly. If you have long hair, plait it so that it will not swing and lash you, or anyone else.

For safety, leave all jewellery at home. Jewellery is a hazard as it can catch on the apparatus, or cause cuts and scratches. Rings can damage the bars.

## First training session

Every gymnastic session starts off with a series of warm-up exercises to get your body ready for work. These are simple activities to get your circulation going, which means your blood moves round your body more quickly and you start to feel warm.

After the warm-up you will do some stretching exercises to help make you more mobile. In the first few sessions the coach will take this slowly and expect you to listen and remember what you are shown.

After the stretching exercises you will start to learn some basic skills. And then to finish the session you will do some simple strength skills, to help you develop enough strength for your size and weight. You will not be allowed on some of the apparatus, until you show good body control when doing these first skills.

## Muscle soreness

Sometimes, a day or two after you have been to the gym, parts of your body will feel sore. Don't be alarmed! This is because some of your muscles have been used in a new way. A warm shower after exercise will help to reduce this.

### Safety tip:

Only do what your coach tells you to do. A gymnasium is not a play area, even though the apparatus looks exciting.

# GYMNASTICS EXERCISES

In this chapter there are some exercises for you to try. They may appear to be very simple but you will find them harder than they look. The key to all of them is good posture so that is the first exercise.

Here you can see two pictures showing good posture and bad posture. The girl in white shows good posture, so copy her example.

## Exercise 1

Stand with your back against a wall and your hands down by your sides. Make sure that your calves, buttocks, shoulders and head are all touching the wall. Now suck in your abdomen. Tighten the muscles in your buttocks to press the lower part of your back towards the wall. Make sure you do not bend your knees. How long can you hold this position for?

When you are sure that you can hold this position properly, try it without the wall to help you. See if you can stand still for 1 minute.

## Exercise 2

Stand with good posture and slowly rise up on to your toes then lower yourself back to the start position. Try doing this 10 times.

Next, try doing it on one leg without wobbling, and then on the other leg. With a little practice you should aim to do 10 toe raises on both legs, 10 toe raises on each leg separately. Do the whole exercise twice.

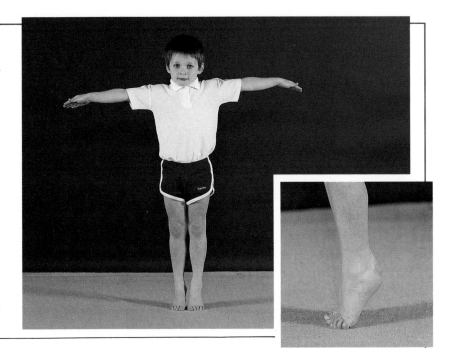

## Exercise 3

Sit up straight, with your abodomen pulled in. Stretch your legs out and rest your hands on the floor behind you. Turn your feet and toes upwards.

Curl your toes downwards as far as you can, then extend your ankles so your feet and toes are stretching. Keep your ankles extended.

Now turn your toes up and separate them. Then, start again. Repeat the exercise 10 times slowly, first with both feet then with one foot at a time.

## Exercise 4

Stand with good posture. (Remember to check the pictures on page 12.) Stretch both arms out in front of you. Turn your hands upwards so that your fingers point to the ceiling and your palms face forwards. Then turn your hands downwards, so your fingers point to the floor. Repeat this 10 times.

Now, with your arms in the same position, try rotating both hands, clockwise and then anticlockwise.

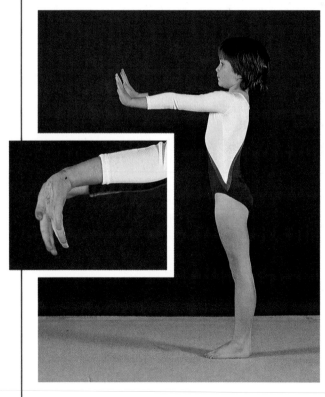

## Exercise 5

Stand against a wall with good posture. Let the palms of your hands touch the wall. Now, keeping both arms straight, swing them slowly up above your head until the back of your hands touch the wall above you. Try this 10 times with a slow swinging action. Then try with alternate arms so that one arm swings up as the other swings back down.

When you are sure you can do this without letting your posture go, take one step away from the wall and try it again.

## Exercise 6

Lie flat on your back with your arms straight and hands resting on top of your thighs. Curl your head and shoulders up, off the floor, keeping your arms straight. Make sure your heels stay firmly on the floor. Hold that position and then lower yourself back down. Repeat 10 times.

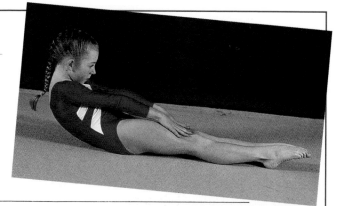

## Exercise 7

Lie on your front with your hands resting on the side of your thighs. Lift your head and shoulders up as high as you can but keep your feet on the floor. Then lower back to your start position. Next, keep your chest and face down and lift your legs off the floor. Repeat this 10 times.

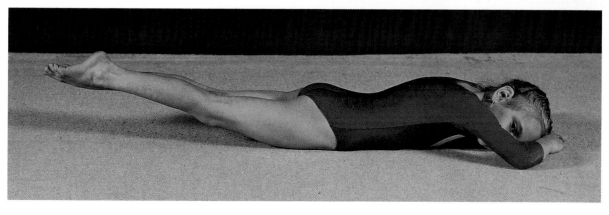

## Exercise 8

Stand against the wall with your hands on your hips and elbows touching the wall. Slowly tilt your body to the right, bending at the waist, as far as you can go. Come slowly back to your start position. Then try bending to the left. Repeat the exercise 10 times to each side.

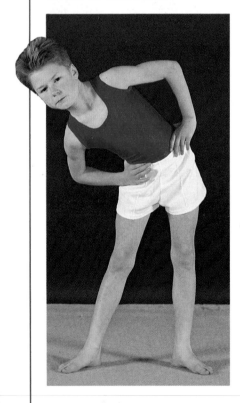

## Exercise 9

Stand facing a wall, with your legs shoulder-width apart and your feet turned slightly out. Put your hands on your hips and fold forwards from the hips, keeping your back and legs straight.

When your chest is parallel to the floor, hold that position, count to two, then come back upright. Repeat this 10 times.

Try exercise 9 again but this time put your feet almost together. As you get used to it, try holding the position for more than a count of two.

## Exercise 10

Let your knees bend as you try the following:

1) Jump up and down on the spot 10 times.
2) Hop 10 times on your right foot.
3) Hop 10 times on your left foot.
4) Run on the spot for a count of ten.
5) Repeat 1) to 4) without stopping for 1 minute.
6) Stop and stand still with perfect posture. Breathe out several times.

Each day, try to build on this until you can do 12 minutes, non-stop.

# SHAPING UP

Here are some examples of shapes used in gymnastics, at all levels. Can you copy them and stay in the exact shape for 3 seconds, then 5 and finally 10 seconds?

Have a go at all the body shapes, then practise those that you can manage. The most difficult ones are on page 20. Ask a friend to help you make the shapes that you find hard. If you practise the first eight regularly, you will be able to make a better attempt at the more difficult ones.

**Front scale**: Stand on one leg and lift the other leg up in front of you. Keep both legs straight. Stretch your arms out to help you balance. Try it on the other leg.

**Back scale**: This should be practised on each leg. Remember to maintain good posture. Keep both legs, especially the one you are standing on, straight.

**'L' sit piked**: Keep your back straight and your arms stretched upwards. Press the back of your knees firmly to the floor.

**'L' sit straddled**: Stretch your feet outwards. Make sure your knees stay facing the ceiling and do not roll inwards.

**'L' lie**: Start by lying flat and lift your legs up into the shape. Your legs must be straight and point directly upwards.

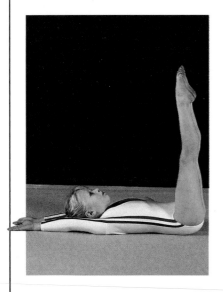

**Shoulder stand**: Press the backs of your hands on the floor above your head. Stretch your feet and legs upwards with your hips off the floor.

**Dish**: Curl your head and shoulders off the floor. At the same time lift up your legs, keeping them straight.

**Arch**: Arch your back and lift and stretch your arms and legs off the floor.

**Back support**: With straight arms and legs, push your hips upwards. Pull in your tummy and buttocks so your body makes a straight line.

**Bridge**: Lie on your back and bend your knees and elbows so your feet and hands are in position. Then push your hips upwards and straighten your arms.

**Front support**: Put your hands shoulder-width apart, with your fingers spread and pointing forwards. Make a straight line from your shoulders to feet.

**Advanced bridge**: Keep your hands flat on the floor and press upwards, from your feet. Straighten your arms and legs, without moving your feet.

**Pike hold**: Put your hands flat on the floor either side of you. Lift yourself from the floor by pushing down on your hands and keeping your arms straight.

**Straddle hold**: Start with a straddle sit and put your hands flat on the floor in front of you. Spread out your fingers. Press down and lift yourself from the floor.

**Russian lever**: This one is very difficult. Try to lift yourself without tipping your shoulders backwards.

# BASIC SKILLS

Some gymnastics skills can be quite simple to learn, but make sure you take your time to really learn the ones that you find difficult. Practise them until you can do them easily. If you have learnt the exercises and shapes earlier in the book you are now ready to learn some skills.

**Practice tip:**

Keep practising the exercises and shapes you have already learnt.

## Half Backward Roll to Stand

Bend your knees and squat down. Keep your back straight and balance on the balls of your feet. Then let your heels drop down and tip backwards. Your seat should touch the floor first, then let yourself roll on to your shoulders.

As you start to roll, bend your elbows and reach your hands back so they touch the floor under your shoulders. At the end of the half roll, your head, shoulders and hands should be on the floor and your hips high in the air.

Then let yourself roll forwards to your starting position. Roll from your shoulders down on to your seat and back through the squat position. Reach forwards with your arms to help you back on to your feet and stand up straight.

# Forward Roll

With your head up, bend your knees and squat down to balance on the balls of your feet.

Reach forwards and put your hands on the floor as you topple over. Tuck your chin on to your chest.

Roll so the back of your head touches the floor first. Push from your feet so the neck, back and seat touch the floor in turn.

Reach forwards with your arms to finish standing up with your heels down and feet slightly apart.

# Backward Roll

Squat down and balance on the balls of your feet. Topple backwards, rolling on to your seat and back.

As you go up on to your shoulders, push with your hands and let your legs carry on over your head.

Straighten your arms as much as you can and push strongly before your feet touch the floor.

As you come back on to your feet, straighten your knees and stand up straight.

## Kick to Handstand

Make sure you have a support when you first try a handstand. Ask a friend to help you or use a wall.

Start by standing with good posture. Stretch your arms up above your head and point one foot in front of you.

Lunge forward by taking a big step on to your front foot and bend that knee. Reach your hands down to the floor with straight arms and your fingers spread.

At the same time swing your kicking leg (the back one) up. As that leg goes up, straighten the stepping leg (the front one), lifting it up alongside the other one.

# Cartwheel

This is a wheeling action of the hands and feet travelling along a straight line. Try to cover as much distance as possible along this line.

Take a large step to the left and bend that knee. Reach down to the ground with your left hand and push off on your left leg. Let your right leg swing up into the air and reach for the floor with your right hand.

Let your legs swing over and as they start to come down the other side, lift your left hand up so you land back on your feet, right foot first.

Start as you did for the handstand but point your stepping foot out to one side. In this example, the cartwheel is to the left.

# PROGRESSIONS

Here are some more skills for you to try. They use all the exercises, shapes and skills you have already learnt but this time, some of the different movements are linked together and there are some new ideas to try.

## Cartwheels

Can you do the following?

- a cartwheel on either side
- a cartwheel on a straight line
- two cartwheels one after the other
- kick harder and only put down your first hand
- only put down your second hand

## Backward rolls

Can you do backward rolls, starting from:

- a piked 'L' sit?

Try to land:

- on one leg
- with legs astride
- on two knees
- on one knee.

## Forward rolls

Can you do forward rolls from different starting positions? Try starting from:

- one leg
- two knees kneeling
- one knee kneeling
- with legs astride.

Try landing:

- on one leg
- in a piked 'L' sit
- in a straddle sit
- in a pike hold
- in a straddle hold.

## Handstands

Once you are balanced in a handstand try to:

- walk on your hands forwards, sideways, and backwards
- bend your arms and go into a forward roll
- come down on to one leg and balance
- move one hand and make a quarter turn into a cartwheel.

# JUMPING AND LANDING

Good jumping begins with good posture
(which you should have practised by now)
and it is your legs which do the work. Try
the following exercise.

Hold your arms out to
your sides and, on your
toes, make 10 jumps.
Keep your chest and seat
in and do not let your arms
flap up and down like
wings.

## How to jump

Start by standing with
good posture, then bend
your knees.  Now jump by
straightening your legs
quickly and at the same
time swing your arms and
reach upwards.  Make sure
you only use your arms and
legs and that your body
stays tight and stretched.

When you are sure you
can do this well, practise
jumping upwards from a
low bench.

## How to land

Landing from your jump
correctly is important as it
helps to prevent injury to
your knees and ankles.

You should only practise
jumping where there is a
firm and even surface to
land on. Land with your
feet slightly apart.  The
balls of your feet should
touch down first, then your
heels and your knees
should bend forwards over
your toes.

## Jumping Progressions

Jumping is one of the most important skills in gymnastics. The higher you can jump, the more time you will have in the air to make a shape or movement perfectly.

Here are some shapes you can make when you jump. They all start with the basic jumping skill.

Tuck jump

Star jump

Pike jump

Straddle jump

# SWINGING AND CLIMBING

If you have a climbing frame or a rope in your garden or a bar in your playground, here are a few useful ideas to try which will keep you safe and make you strong.

## Rope Climbing

1  Try climbing a rope using both your hands and your feet.
2. Then try climbing using just your arms.

## Swinging

1. Swing with straight legs.
2. Hang on the bar and 'walk', one hand at a time, along it.
3. Make a half turn while hanging then make a full turn.
4. Hang straight, then pull your knees right up to your chest and hold them there.
5. Hang on the bar and pull yourself up by bending your elbows. See if you can pull yourself up enough to look over the bar.

### Safety tips:
- Only let go of the bar on a backward swing, so you can see the ground and your landing spot.
- Always climb back down a rope, never slide down.

# GYM SAFETY

Safety in a gym is really a question of common sense and showing consideration for other people. If you stick to a few simple rules you should be able to prevent silly accidents and enjoy your gymnastics in safety.

## Ten Tips for Safe Gymnastics

1. Be alert by getting enough sleep.
2. Provide energy for your body by eating the correct foods.
3. Avoid eating big meals before training.
4. Dress correctly.
5. Keep your clothing and training equipment in good condition.
6. Leave jewellery at home.
7. Listen carefully to instructions and only do what you are told.
8. Check the apparatus before use.
9. Never walk underneath or over apparatus.
10. Obey the rules of your gym.

# GOING FURTHER

Classes are available for everyone at clubs and sports centres throughout the country, and learning gymnastics is an exciting way to become physically fit and active. When you have chosen the type of gymnastics that interests you and have joined a club, you can start to take part in award schemes and earn your badges and certificates. As you get more skilful you might like to take part in competitions.

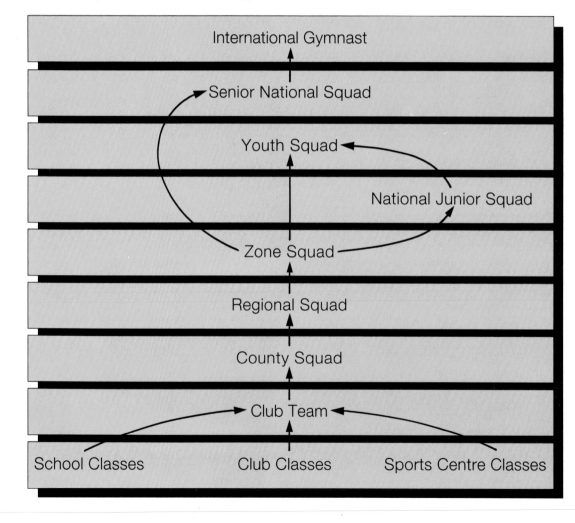

At first the competitions will be in your own club and then against other local clubs. If you like competing and your gymnastics skills continue to improve, there is a ladder to the top.

Of course, to make your way up the ladder will mean years of hard work at home and in the gym. But for now, choose which sort of gymnastics you want to learn, find a class or club to join, and enjoy your gymnastics.

# INDEX

advanced bridge, 20
apparatus, 7,8
arch, 19

back scale, 17
back support, 19
backward roll, 22, 25
beam, 7
bridge, 19
British Amateur
  Gymnastics
  Association, 9
broad horse, 7

cartwheel, 24, 25
clothing, 10

dish, 19

exercises, 11, 12–16

floor, 7, 8
footware, 10
forward roll, 22, 25
front scale, 17
front support, 19

Greece, 3
group work, 5
gym clubs, 9, 30, 31

hair, 10
half backward roll, 21
handstand, 23, 25
high bar, 8

Jahn, Friedrich
  Ludwig, 3
jewellery, 10
jumping, 26, 27

landing, 26
lie, 18
Ling, Pierre, 3
long horse, 8

pair work, 5
parallel bars, 8
pike, 18
pike hold, 20
pommel horse, 8

rings, 8
rope climbing, 28
Russian lever, 20

safety, 29
sit, 18
shoulder stand, 18
straddle, 18
straddle hold, 20

swinging, 28

training, 11
tumbling, 5

uneven bars, 7

This edition published 1994 by Diamond Books
77–85 Fulham Palace Road
Hammersmith, London W6 8JB

First published in Great Britain 1992

© HarperCollinsPublishers 1992

ISBN 0 261 66 470-0

Printed and bound in Italy

PHOTO ACKNOWLEDGEMENTS

Mary Evans Picture Library: 3
All other photographs © Eileen Langsley, Supersport
Photographs 1992